# BREAK FREE FROM ANXIETY

## How to Control Anxiety, Panic Attacks and Negative Emotions Before They Control You!

Esmeralda Franco-Mansilla, MD/MACP

Published by Manzillana Press
London, Ontario, Canada

DISCLAIMER:

*Break Free from Anxiety* is strictly for educational, informational, guidance, and motivational purposes.

The author and publisher are not offering it as legal, medical, psychological or other professional services advice. Nor should it be construed as such.

While best efforts and research were used while preparing this book, the author and publisher make no representations or warranties of any kind, nor do they assume liability of any kind with respect to the accuracy or completeness of its contents.

The author and publisher specifically disclaim any implied warranties of merchantability or fitness of use for a particular purpose.

Neither the author nor the publisher shall be held liable or responsible to any person or entity with respect to any loss or incidental or consequential damages caused, or alleged to have been caused, directly or indirectly, by the information or strategies contained herein, as the advice and strategies contained herein might not be suitable for an individual's unique situation.

The information contained within was written to help you make educated, well-informed decisions based on your specific needs. Therefore, you are responsible for your own choices and actions, and should seek the services of a competent professional before or taking any action.

# CONTENTS

# Dedication

I wish to dedicate this book to my husband, my two daughters, and my son who always look at me with respect, belief and love in their eyes.

I thank my editor Mary Jo Stresky who worked hard to make my manuscript become a gem.

I also want to mention those individuals who didn't believe in my dreams and goals as they made me strive to become a better person, and to write this book that can help others overcome their struggles with anxiety, panic attacks and depression.

# INTRODUCTION

You're probably reading this book because anxiety and/or panic attacks are severely crippling your personal life, your career, and your relationships.

Within *Break Free from Anxiety* I'll be discussing...

- how to discern between anxiety, fear and stress so you can determine the best treatment protocol to become calmer, anxiety-free, and more self-confident.
- the different kinds of pressure and stress people experience in their daily life.
- how to achieve optimal health by first recognizing your problems. Then how to deal with them by utilizing my strategies to greatly reduce or eliminate the stressors that try to control my client's lives.
- why anxiety takes a toll on your well-being.
- why fear can cripple you emotionally, physically, and psychologically.

My objective for writing this book is to provide *tools and exercises* to *identify* your particular kind of anxiety, and the *strategies* to control it.

I'll be providing information, encouragement and support while introducing new techniques and strategies to utilize at your own pace.

The good news is there's no 'expiration date' as you'll be able to use these tools throughout your entire life!

Routinely practicing my guidelines and methodologies, then incorporating them into your daily lifestyle, can greatly improve your physical, emotional and psychological well-being. More importantly, I'll provide practical steps to help you *control your emotions instead of having them control you!*

I also wrote this book to give you wisdom and awareness, a greater sense of belonging, and renewed strength as you have many wonderful years still ahead of you.

Quelling your emotional storms to get you safely back to shore will give you the serenity to live your life with grace, fortitude and conviction.

As you immerse yourself in understanding the complexities of your emotions, you'll acquire the power and knowledge to improve your energy, become healthier, and enjoy your life in a way you never could have imagined.

Thank you from the bottom of my heart for joining me on your journey to wellness!

Esmeralda Franco-Mansilla, MD/MACP

# Chapter One

## *ANXIETY IS A GLOBAL PANDEMIC*

*"Some people have called anxiety the Disease of the 21st Century; and on an anecdotal level, it's easy to understand how someone might think anxiety worthy of the title.*
*We've all experienced it at one time or another – that horrible feeling when the whole world seems to be crashing down on us.*
*But is humanity truly in the grips of an anxiety epidemic?"*
**~Georgy Dvorsky, Canadian bioethicist**

Whether hidden from others, or out in the open, anxiety is a global affliction. Psychological issues manifest differently from culture to culture.

For people living abroad, their cultural values, beliefs and traditions can conflict with the people in their community.

Cultural factors influence how individuals perceive and express their psychological distress.

To illustrate, when diagnosing mental from physical conditions, Eastern or Middle-Eastern cultures view mind and body as being integrated with social context. Since mental disorders are viewed as one entity, people feel ashamed and have difficulty sharing or discussing their symptoms in order to be healed.

Whereas in more Western cultures like the U.S., a diagnosis of a mental disorder differs from a physical condition, so each one is attended to separately and more openly.

There are many factors that contribute to anxiety in different societies, among which are vulnerability, traumatic past or present events, and living a hectic lifestyle.

Biological factors, personality types, patterns of negative behavior, and a history of family members managing high volumes of daily stress are common sources of anxiety. Though anxiety can pass from generation to generation, it's typically transgenerational rather than hereditary.

Living in a distressing, negative environment also contributes to this disorder.

However, it's known that for people who are surrounded by peaceful surroundings, and have supportive relationships with their family members, the risk factors for having anxiety disorder significantly decrease.

Some studies suggest a strong correlation between vulnerability and stress in the development of mental disorders. In some individuals, vulnerability is the susceptibility to generating a mental or behavioral disorder when exposed to stress. Whereas stress is the unpleasant interpretation of everyday life events where, for example, a regular day job and tasks become a burden.

## Fear's Repository

Have you ever wondered what happens to fears collected from hostile events?

Fear is a negative thought generated when facing possible or actual threatening situations. The difference between how you, versus someone else, respond to those thoughts is based on character make-up and decision-making abilities.

For example, you observe an event via all five senses (sight, sound, smell, taste and touch). That experience is then carried by your senses to your brain where a reaction or thought is created. Your thoughts then become feelings, beliefs and actions that can morph into either fear that paralyzes you, or positive thoughts that incite you to take action.

This doesn't mean you won't ever feel fear, or have wrong perceptions of a situation; it's how you choose to express then deal with them.

Without realizing it, you feel different levels of fear every single day. Some might even be beneficial, such as warning you a car is about to hit your car, or a dog is about to attack.

However, my focus is on the kind of fear that paralyzes you to the point of not allowing you to function properly.

### A Quick Mini-Exercise

An affirmative exercise for preventing out-of-control fear is to think *all intrusive thoughts, be gone from my mind!* as often as possible as it will help you become more confident, have more peace of mind, and be in more in control of your life.

Because distressing thoughts fade when they're replaced with constructive one, in essence you're replacing a bad thought habit with a good one.

## How to Handle Anxiety

The process of identifying problems can be both challenging and intriguing. Some people become distraught by not knowing how to cope with debilitating emotions. But knowing how to identify what's causing them can help you effectively deal with them.

What you'll learn in this book will help you quickly identify symptoms such as heavy, fast breathing, sweaty palms, and erratic thoughts. Conversely, not being able to identify the signs and symptoms can lead to an anxiety or panic attack if not controlled as early as possible.

*Don't worry!* The more you learn about what causes your anxiousness or panic attacks, the easier you'll be able to access the information stored in your mind, even during a crisis.

Your moods and behavior will become calmer and more peaceful because you'll apply what you've learned to your healing.

Over time you'll notice a considerable change from how you used to handle anxiety, to how you now can handle it more effectively and with less stress.

## Choosing the Right Path

People are born into this world without anxiety, stress or fear. But as they grow older, they have good and bad experiences that can cause anxiety.

When you were a baby you had "baby thoughts." As a mature adult, your thoughts are more elaborate based on your overall experience, and your reasoning skills to make logical decisions.

Memories of past experiences often help you choose what to see, perceive and believe about the outside world.

Your mind becomes empowered to create your path you'll be walking for the rest of your life.

Imagine two people driving to Toronto, Canada from New York City. By the time they reach Toronto, each person will have a different story based on the route they choose to take, and the different sights, sounds and people they experience along the way.

Likewise, you choose the path for your life's journey. You choose your experiences, and whether you'll interact negatively or positively based on your observations and points of view.

But first, it's important to understand the difference between anxiety, depression, panic and fear so you can choose the proper action to regain control over your life!

*NOTE: I've included exercises in the upcoming chapters to help you question, then face, some of the problems you're having so you can determine a proper method of treatment. Or maybe just knowing you're not alone, that you're normal and VERY OKAY, can be enough to help!*

# Chapter Two

## *WHAT EXACTLY IS ANXIETY?*

**"The best thing about the future is that it comes only one day at a time."**
**~Dean Acheson, American statesman and attorney**

Anxiety is a universal issue that's spiraling out of control. According to the National Institute of Mental Health (NIMH), anxiety disorders affect 40 million of people in the United States annually. Sadly, only a small percentage receive proper treatment because they're often misdiagnosed, or are afraid to admit they're experiencing problems.

A report from the Public Health Agency of Canada states that anxiety disorders affect 12% of the population (almost 13 million people!).

Similarly, in Colombia, South America where I practiced before moving to Canada, anxiety disorders are frequently reported at 19.3% of the lifetime prevalence rates, which means approximately eight million people are affected.

Almost ten million people in Western Europe, including the United Kingdom, and more than seven million people in South Africa, have anxiety disorders. Combining those numbers, you'll see that 78 million people from those countries are afflicted with a life-controlling condition. However, the statistics can be even higher because many people are underdiagnosed or misdiagnosed.

Depression is similar, or even worse, as it can cause more harm in the individual, their loved ones, and society in general. Plus it can create thoughts of suicide.

The above data show that anxiety disorders and panic attacks can occur to anyone of any age, gender, educational level, culture, or even religious belief as it is a non-discerning condition that fortunately can be treated if diagnosed early enough.

(For more statistics by country
for anxiety disorders you can visit:
http://www.rightdiagnosis.com/a/anxiety_disorders/stat
s-country.htm)

## Identifying Your Anxiety, Emotions and Feelings

*"Courage is about learning how to function despite the fear, to put aside your instincts to run or give in completely to the anger born from fear. Courage is about using your brain and your heart when every cell of your body is screaming at you to fight or flee - and then following through on what you believe is the right thing to do."*
**~Jim Butcher,** author of *Ghost Story*

You've probably struggled to find a name for your rollercoaster emotions and anxieties. You might have even visited a physician or a therapist like myself who discounted them, couldn't pinpoint them, or prescribed drugs to calm them, which only served to numb you, or made you even more anxious.

The name for that feeling of apprehensiveness, fear, tension and being on pins and needles is called *anxiety*, which can come in many forms.

The definition of anxiety is often used interchangeably with fear, stress and panic attacks. Fear is what you think; stress is the way your body responds or adjusts to pressure. And according to Edmund Bourne, PhD, in his *Anxiety and Phobia Workbook*, panic attacks are "...abrupt, unexpected episodes of intense fear and physical symptoms as a response to a situation, event or people."

Emotions are biochemical reactions in your body, whereas feelings are mental associations after experiencing those emotions. Your physical body reacts to an emotion either as an emotional arousal, or by regulating the reaction by assigning meaning to the emotion which involves a thought process.

### *Anxiety*

Anxiety is a physical manifestation of your fears (the cognitive process or construction of thoughts).

Understanding that your thoughts create worries takes you one step closer to overcoming then solving your problems.

Anxiety…

- is a painful or apprehensive uneasiness and self-doubt about having the capacity to cope with abnormal fears or dislikes.

- manifests as physical symptoms such as teeth grinding, stuttering, gastritis, cardiovascular and respiratory complaints (such as heart palpitations), headaches, profuse sweating, or sweaty palms (just to mention a few) that can erode your self-confidence or self-esteem.

- prevents effective or realistic ways to prepare for upcoming events.

- creates awkward sensations in the body, such as butterflies in your stomach, feeling antsy, nervous twitches, or a paranoid feeling like someone is watching that causes you to walk faster or run (aka: the fight-or-flight response).

- can make you feel like something is missing, but you can't put your finger on what it is.

- can make you feel incomplete or empty.

- can prevent you from being focused on your work because you're constantly thinking of everything on your to-do list.

It's as though the ON switch in your mind is broken, and your thoughts spin faster and faster to the point of losing control.

### *Emotions*

Emotions are a physiological and chemical response to external influences, such as the death of a loved one, the loss of a job, abandonment, rejection.
In other words, any kind of environmental, mental or physical stimulation that can create an imbalanced state of mental being.

The state of a person's emotions can scientifically be determined by observing their body language (tension, arms tightly folded, hands clenched, anger or happiness in their eyes, etc.), blood flow, and brain activity.

### *Feelings*

Feelings are triggered by subconscious responses to one's emotions based on their experiences, belief system and memories.

For example, a child who's been bullied can re-feel that experience as a teen because of the memory of the trauma. An adult can feel elated when they get a promotion at work because they remember getting a medal in high school for track and field.

## Signs and Symptoms

Some practitioners think the cause of anxiety is from organic sources such as an imbalance in the brain's chemistry. While others think it's caused by other common factors such as lifestyle, unsatisfactory or difficult relationships, and/or the individual's cultural struggles they face after emigrating to another land, just to mention a few.

A general state of anxiety can escalate to an anxiety disorder, which is often triggered by outside influences.

Also "negative auto-talk" (a repetitive pattern of convincing yourself that the worst will happen) can be a contributing factor. Over time, this pattern or way of thinking becomes a habitual perception you perform on "auto-pilot," and controls everything you do, say or feel.

Individuals with general anxiety disorders can exhibit the following signs and symptoms:

- anxiousness
- restlessness
- lightheadedness
- trembling hands
- tics or twitches
- lack of concentration
- excessive urination
- dizziness
- difficulty in breathing
- irritability
- nervous foot or finger tapping
- pacing the floor with worrisome thoughts
- fearful of leaving their house
- terrified of driving in traffic, crowds, or even small groups of people
- insomnia
- fatigue and lethargy
- unexplained aches and pains
- jumping at loud noises
- worrying too much about general everyday issues

Remembering that anxiety is a state of distress caused by emotions and feelings, there are techniques can be applied before or after your emotions escalate:

- recognizing and accepting the presence of anxiety
- developing tools for self-observation and self-talk
- maintaining self-monitoring via a daily routine agenda (which I'll discuss later)
- reinforcing your mind with positive, constructive thoughts
- breathing exercises to calm the body and mind

Recognizing, then accepting the presence of, anxiety is crucial in diagnosing anxiety disorders.

You might deny your symptoms by justifying them as being a part of your personality, especially if you have to step out of your comfort zone to acknowledge them.

Instead of fighting the facts, owning that you have a problem that millions of people experience on a daily basis can be a first step toward mental wellness.

Accepting the fact that you have an emotional anxiety disorder doesn't mean you have to resign yourself to living with it permanently. To the contrary.

*The main point here is to recognize that anxiety isn't a catastrophic condition, nor should you be judged for having it.*

## You Are *Not* Alone!

*"Engaging in meditative self-reflection and gaining increased control of inner experiences provides a person with a sense of control over fear and trembling and the chaos of life."*
~**Kilroy J. Oldster**, author of *Dead Toad Scrolls*

What could be the worst thing that could happen by owning your anxiety? That you get better? That you're relieved that others have it as well?

***That you can get through your days knowing you're in control of your emotions rather than them being in control of you?***

Everyone experiences anxiety at some point in their life. A powerful emotion, it can rear its ugly head at any moment, and negatively affect you if it's not dealt with quickly and properly. This disturbing emotional state can take hold of you, then stay for years or decades to erode your identity, self-confidence, and self-esteem. So it's up to you to decide whether to allow it in... or let it go.

I personally can relate to how anxiety can take a stronghold on people's lives. During my first year as a medical student, I started experiencing feelings of uneasiness. I thought it was a normal response because of my hefty academic load, and only sleeping for only a few hours in between working on assignments.

One day while participating in the delivery of a newborn in the obstetrics room, I had an *acute anxiety attack* and passed out.

Although other people were in attendance, I apparently was terrified that I'd have to deliver the baby by myself.

Over time, the more I became exposed to this kind of situation in a teaching environment, the more confident I became. But it took the entire semester to finally defeat my anxieties. If I'd had someone to talk to about my fears, I might have learned how to control them instead of them controlling me.

## You Are Only Human!

Anxiety affects people struggling with everyday living. Tension associated with fear, phobias, sleep disturbances, and restlessness can cripple even the most stalwart of individuals.

Many people who give the outward appearance of being strong, cool, and in control actually suffer inwardly from several anxiety and panic attacks to the point of not being to perform effectively or even at all.

People tend to forget that famous people are just human beings. For example, the iconic Oprah Winfrey, who comes across as being comfortable in her own skin, knew she was in trouble when she started losing control of her emotions during the filming of *The Butler.*

> *"I was in the middle of doing voiceovers. And I remember closing my eyes in between each page because looking at the page and the words at the same time was too much stimulation for my brain."*

Emma Stone, who won an Oscar in 2017 for Best Actress for her strong performance in the musical, *La-La-Land*, has experienced crippling shyness, anxiety, panic attacks and even phobias the majority of her life:

> *"The first time I had a panic attack I was sitting in my friend's house, and I thought the house was burning down. I called my mom and she brought me home, and for the next three years it just would not stop. I would go to the nurse at lunch most days and just wring my hands.*
> *I would ask my mom to tell me exactly how the day was going to be, then ask again 30 seconds later. I just needed to know that no one was going to die and nothing was going to change."*

Donny Osmond, from the famed Osmond Family singers, who struck out on his own many years ago, said:

> *"Well, unless you've suffered from panic attacks and social anxiety disorders, which is what I was diagnosed as having, it's hard to explain it. But you go on stage knowing you're actually physically going to die. You will keel over and die."*

Multiple award-winning actress, Glenn Close, has openly discussed her battle with depression, and how certain mental conditions exist in her family:

> *"It's amazing when you open up, how receptive others are and how you're not alone," she says. "The best way to change someone's attitude is to hear a story, and hear a story from someone who looks just like them."*

Reports of his life-long struggle with anxiety and depression surfaced after Michael Jackson's death.

The great author, John Steinbeck, and the sixteenth president of the United States, Abraham Lincoln (yes, even the much-revered Abe!!) were treated for anxiety and severe depression.

The iconic singer, Barbara Streisand, has been known to take anxiety medication before she performs.

And who would think that the handsome, charismatic and famous soccer player, David Beckham, plays Legos to get his emotions under control?

**Does it help to know that you're not alone?**

## Learning to Share Your Anxieties with Others

> **"You own everything that happened to you.**
> **Tell your stories.**
> **If people wanted you to write warmly about**
> **them, they should have behaved better."**
> **~Anne Lamott, author of *Bird by Bird: Some***
> ***Instructions on Writing and Life***

The following two case studies are examples of individuals who participated in online group therapy sessions about social anxiety disorder.

All of the participants, including myself, were each other's "therapists" while discussing the issues.

In addition to sharing their anxieties, these two men listened intently to the other participants' issues in order to find solutions to their own problems.

Both Daniel and David were amenable to sharing their feelings with the group. They were intelligent individuals who seemed comfortable in their surroundings, and treated others in the group with great kindness.

Participating in an online group where they didn't have to physically face each other afforded them the opportunity to speak freely, and without censoring their emotions and experiences.

(The purpose behind sharing these case studies with you is to help you realize that you're not alone. You'll note that most of their comments are based on social interactions – what David calls "social shyness" – which is a leading cause of anxiety.)

*NOTE: The names of these individuals were changed to protect their identities.*

# CASE STUDY ONE: DANIEL

Daniel said that although he was quiet and reserved, he was relatively social in high school, college and at his first job. However, while at that job he experienced critical bosses, and lost a sales job because he couldn't make cold calls:

> *"I got stressed out and stopped making calls. Ever since then I'm afraid of groups and meeting new people. I also get very stressed about going out."*

Whenever Daniel was at social meetings, he'd wonder what he could talk about since he felt he didn't have anything interesting to say:

*"I don't think people will like me much. My mind goes blank. I get stressed and nervous and want to get out of there. Then I feel relieved when I get home where I'd rather watch movies and television."*

When he finally accepted help, the therapist focused on determining the extent of his social anxiety and social shyness:

*"I think I expect too much of myself. I judge myself, and then I think that others judge me the same way when they meet me."*

Talking during these online sessions helped Daniel see that he indeed was too hard on himself. And that other people don't have big expectations or judgments about him, which helped him break through the fear of being in social settings so he could just be himself.

## CASE STUDY TWO: DAVID

During his initial stage of sharing, David confessed being fearful of groups and meeting new people:

*"My family lives in the East, so I'm alone here. I get very stressed about going out. I try to think about what I would talk about, but I don't have anything interesting to say.*

*I used to drink to socialize because I thought people would like me. But then it became a problem."*

David was open to discussing his social anxiety, and what worried him the most, so he could learn how to control his emotions:

*"Though I still see myself as a recovering social-phobic, I've put much of my social anxiety behind me. I was very nervous in public, especially at parties, because it seemed everyone in the room could make conversation with others, while I thought I had nothing of value to say. So unlike others I know who have social shyness, the anxiety often caused me to talk too much. The next day I'd feel so guilty and stupid that I wouldn't attend anything for fear of making a fool of myself."*

During his sessions, David worked through the process of treating his social anxiety. His significant improvement created a positive impact on the entire group.

If you choose to become involved in group therapy, your goal should be to comfortably and spontaneously participate in sharing in order to get the most from the experience. For instance, although David clearly expressed his fears of not being liked if he joined a social gathering, he realized his strong emotions were interfering with the prospects of having a normal life.

Social anxiety can cause embarrassment as it's a strong fear of being judged by or doing things in front of others.

Though social phobia or anxiety can run in families, the overall cause behind this disorder is still unknown.

Some researchers have found that some parts of the brain play a part in fear and anxiety. Whereas others are searching for answers to why stress and environmental factors might be involved as possible causes. (National Institute of Mental Health, 2012)

After an afflicted individual willingly goes to treatment sessions for several weeks, they'll begin to notice a more solid structure to their personality, more positive outcomes of any endeavor, and a more rewarding sense of achievement and completeness.

Sharing your problems with people who have the same difficulties can help you stop being so hard on yourself. It might be intimidating at first to reach out if you're not sure what to do or say, which can cause you to become anxious and have negative thoughts.

As Daniel stated, "Maybe there's some way for us to break through the fear."

Both Daniel and David stated that participating in therapeutic sessions became critical to their well-being as they could first identify, then face their core fears. They realized they'd been hiding their fears their entire lives, often agonizing in silence because they were too embarrassed to share them.

Therefore, understanding how to control their emotions, thoughts and perceptions instilled hope that they could live much happier, healthier and fruitful lives!

Some of the other participants also indicated their mind sometimes goes blank or wanders. Or they have many thoughts swirling in their mind at the same time. They were worried they couldn't follow a conversation whenever in a social gathering, so they made excuses not go.

## Owning Your Fears in Order to Take Control of Them

Mandy, another participant in the group, shared that she had irrational fears that prevented her from being authentic in social settings:

> *"I'm looking forward to finishing this therapy with encouraging and practical advice to follow through with it for the rest of my life. The [group] provided me with tools to use. With those tools, I am capable of doing and achieving the best for me. With that in mind, I'll feel energized to defeat the tricks my mind tries to play on me."*

Like other individuals suffering from any type of anxiety disorder who've learned to control their fears, you can learn the same skills as long as you keep practicing my suggested strategies within this book, *which includes taking responsibility for and ownership of your fears.*

For example, your strategy could include things like...

- I'm aware of the demands my irrational fears place on me.

- I will make a practice of recognizing my anxieties in order to instantly stop them.

- I will constantly remind myself that I'm not alone on this journey to healing.

- Many people like Daniel and David are struggling with the same problems. If they can control their strong emotions, I'm capable of doing that as well.

- My next step is to stay ahead of my fears, move forward to live fully in the present, and remind myself that out-of-control anxiety is paralyzing, impractical and ineffective.

Instead of waiting too long to figure out what's going on, and why you can't express your feelings, it's best to get help from a licensed practitioner specializing in anxiety disorders.

## *Exercise 1: Accentuate the Positive*

As an example from personal experience, breaking work projects into smaller pieces prevents the larger picture from overwhelming me. It helps me to stay focused so I can move forward from unrealistic to realistic goals.

Achieving my target goals by doing things one step at a time helps my new thoughts, feelings and actions to become second nature, and helps me become the positive person I want to be.

(The side comments are how I'd answer these questions to help you come up with your own.)

*Negative Things Going Against You*

What makes you feel vulnerable (i.e., I repeat the same thoughts over and over)?

_______________________________________

_______________________________________

_______________________________________

_______________________________________

What were some triggers for your most recent anxiety episode (i.e., I recently met an old friend at a social gathering, which caused me to recall a negative experience)?

_______________________________________

_______________________________________

_______________________________________

_______________________________________

What kinds of self-doubt are you experiencing at the moment (i.e., I'm not good enough while others are exceptionally good)?

_______________________________________

_______________________________________

_______________________________________

_______________________________________

What kinds of self-talk keep your self-doubt alive (i.e., I don't have the confidence to reach specific goals)?

_______________________________________

_______________________________________

_______________________________________

_______________________________________

What things about your personality don't you like and would like to change (i.e., I chatter too much in social settings; I talk over people instead of listening to them; I'm a terrible procrastinator, etc.)?

_______________________________________________

_______________________________________________

_______________________________________________

_______________________________________________

*Positive Things Working for You*

What makes you feel confident, safe and secure (i.e., I can accomplish my plan for the day. I'm in control of strong emotions I had failed to notice before.)

_______________________________________________

_______________________________________________

_______________________________________________

What things do you like about your personality (i.e., I'm determined in spite of being afraid. I smile at others, which makes me a gentler, kinder person)?

_______________________________________________

_______________________________________________

_______________________________________________

What kinds of skills and strengths help you achieve good results at home and at work (i.e., following the examples and exercises in this book has proven that I achieve goals, and that I'm a reliable, friendly person)?

_______________________________________________

_______________________________________________

_______________________________________________

What kinds of positive self-talk keep self-doubt away (i.e., I'll begin with just one baby step at a time. Then I'll validate this step as the first brick to building my wall of faith.)

_______________________________________________

_______________________________________________

_______________________________________________

_______________________________________________

What kinds of positive compliments have people made about you (i.e., my friend invited me to another social gathering because we had a great time together, which is positive evidence that I'm not boring.

Another example is my supervisor commended me for my presentation as it was succinct and applicable to the workplace, which is positive evidence that I'm capable of putting my skills into practice.)

_______________________________________________

_______________________________________________

_______________________________________________

_______________________________________________

The purpose of this exercise is to show you that the lack of self-confidence is often manifested by your fears and self-doubt. When in reality you have more strength, courage, skills, talent and creativity than you probably realize.

So take time to think about the things you like about yourself, and the things you want to change. Then create a plan to tackle them one at a time.

# Chapter Three

## *A THORN IN PEOPLE'S SIDES*

**"What worries you, masters you."**
**~John Locke, 17th Century English philosopher**

## Anxiety is Not a New Kid on the Block

Anxiety has caused problems for people since the beginning of time.

In the Book of Genesis in the Bible, anxiousness and nervousness arose during the Fall of Eden.

Think about it: from the moment the Serpent enters the scene, all kinds of chaos, suspicions and even threats caused self-doubt and anxiety between Adam and Eve, and even their children, Cain and Abel (which led to Cain murdering his brother.

Of course that's an extreme example. But anxiety, panic, and even phobias can cause people to do things they normally wouldn't do.)

Throughout history terrifying events such as war, earthquakes, tsunamis, disease, or separation from loved ones have caused great bouts of anxiety and depression.

Even failing an exam or losing a job can cause anxiety to bubble to the surface, thereby hampering a person's ability to focus and function.

This feeling of uneasiness or restlessness is the common denominator in the way a person behaves when experiencing anxiety.

## What Scientists, Psychologists and Psychotherapists Look For

Until the past few years, anxiety had been considered as an out-of-control emotion expressed by physical responses (racing heart, increased breathing, sweaty hands, queasy stomach, etc.).

However, I firmly believe something more paramount is responsible for an individual's reactions, which is what you're about to discover.

*Would it help to know your thoughts are the main culprits behind your anxiety?*

For many years scientists and researchers have tried to find the underlying causes of anxiety in order to develop proper medical and psychological protocols.

However, little attention was given to cognitive thought processes (how an individual acquires knowledge through experiences, senses, and thoughts)... until now.

It can be difficult for people to describe their symptoms well enough to make a proper diagnosis. Because their mind becomes over-saturated with thoughts of a threatening nature, their descriptions can be vague and confusing.

A difficult challenge I often face as a psychotherapist is when an outwardly calm, controlled and happy person comes to me for help.

It's difficult because three or four sessions are typically needed for their problems to rise to the surface. It's challenging because it can be easy to become lost in the diversity of a bright mind, and to lose focus because they want to chatter (typically because they're nervous) as opposed to tackling their issues.

A skillful therapist won't lose focus on the task at hand. They make their patient feel comfortable by steadily building a supportive rapport, then tactfully remind their patient they've come to them for a particular reason.

The reason behind their issues isn't usually a surprise as past emotional injuries are often hidden underneath their happy, extroverted and outgoing façade.

Once I peel back the "happy" layer to get to the root cause of their anxieties, it's often revealed that their problems manifested their anxiety, or are a precursor to depression. After a few more sessions, the patient finally realizes the real reason behind their visits. I applaud them for being wise enough to seek assistance – and to keep coming to sessions – because something obviously was off-kilter.

## It's All About Perceptions and Attitudes

*"Man is not worried by real problems*
*so much as by his imagined anxieties*
*about real problems."*
**~Epictetus, ancient Greek philosopher**

Studies have demonstrated the relationship between behavior, mental attitude and happiness. As an illustration, when a very dear client was diagnosed with breast cancer, she reacted positively when she received the bad news of only having a five-year chance of survival. Not only did she live the full five years, she surpassed it by living eight years with a good quality of life right up until the day she passed.

On the other hand, one of my clients expressed her concern of developing cancer every time she visited my office.

Though initially she didn't have the disease, she eventually developed it and died quickly, in contrast to my client whose positive attitude helped her live almost double the expected time.

One might say her negative thoughts might have manifested the disease (a topic that causes a lot of conversation and controversy). However, there's a great deal of new research about how positive versus negative thoughts can affect a person's mental and physical health.

It's believed that 85% of physical illnesses are manifested by the mind. For example, many years ago, gastric ulcers were strictly regarded as a physical disease caused by "organic issues."

While studies suggested gastritis was produced by *helicobacter pylori bacterium*, they didn't focus on stress or psychosomatic factors being a causal factor.

Today's advanced research studies suggest chronic stress can severely affect your health. And that without well-balanced management, you can develop one or more anxiety disorders.

Fortunately, researchers have found direct correlation between behavior, attitude and happiness. Therefore, it's my firm belief that changing negative attitudes, behaviors and habits to positive ones will lead you to a much happier, healthier and fruitful life!

## Exercise 2: Defining Your Feelings

In my practice I ask my clients to identify, then describe, what types of thoughts occur prior to experiencing symptoms of discomfort. Providing answers to these kinds of questions might seem difficult. But it can become easier with a little practice.

In this exercise I want you to close your eyes and focus on the thoughts you're having at this very moment. Then write down individual words or sentences that describe those thoughts:

_______________________________________________

_______________________________________________

_______________________________________________

_______________________________________________

_______________________________________________

Describe how those thoughts make you feel (anxious, calm, worried, happy, depressed, etc.):

---

---

---

---

---

What kinds of images came to you while you had your eyes closed?

---

---

---

---

---

Quite often individuals don't realize they're having certain feelings or emotions until they see actual words such as angry, bitter, alone, fearful, anxious, etc.

Writing your feelings down can define them to help you find the right method to tackle, then control them before they control you.

# Chapter Four

## *DISTINGUISHING BETWEEN ANXIETY, FEAR AND STRESS*

**"Pain nourishes courage. You can't be brave if you have only had wonderful things happen to you."**
**~Mary Tyler Moore, American actress**
**(1936-2017)**

## Different Kinds of Anxiety Personas

There are specific groups of people who tend to experience anxiety:

1. Group one can complete many activities and responsibilities without feeling stressed because they have excellent time management and coping skills. They go through their day feeling calm, happy and productive. At the end of the day they feel proud of their accomplishments.

2. Group two completes the same activities. However, if they see a threat in an assignment, the stress response could trigger anxiety while performing their daily tasks.

   They begin to feel overwhelmed, worried, edgy, jumpy, apprehensive, nervous and even frightened. Many times they don't notice emotional manifestations because they accept that's just the way they are. They'll often avoid doing a task because of how it makes them feel.

3. Group three have a tendency toward procrastination, or avoiding their assignments or responsibilities, because they lack time management skills.

Whatever emotions or feelings (i.e., anxiety, fear, insecurities, etc.) individuals in groups two and three might experience, they're more prone to developing an anxiety disorder than group one.

Regardless of which group you belong to, the point is to not allow stress to gain control over your life, and how you react to people and situations.

The more you give in to your emotions, the more stress hormones your body produces (i.e., cortisol). You'll remain in a constant state of hyperawareness, and your body odor (sweat) might increase due to a physical response.

In fact, you might have been experiencing the symptoms for a such a long period of time that you don't realize they're occurring.

For example, a mother becomes worried because it's late and her teenage daughters have yet to arrive home. She paces the kitchen floor while watching the clock tick the minutes away.

Restless and fearful over what could have happened causes her heart to pound, her hands to shake, and she experiences shortness of breath.

In great distress, and unable to wait any longer, she puts on a jacket and shoes.

As she starts walking down the driveway to go search for her daughters, she sees them walking toward her, laughing as though they didn't have a care in the world.

One daughter says, "Hey Mom, we decided to walk home since we were only a few blocks away. What are you doing out here?"

Noticing that her mother looks fearful and pale, the other daughter asks, "Mom, are you okay?"

Speechless and confused, the mother realizes she over-dramatized the situation based on unknown factors. Her fear and negative perceptions of what might have been versus the reality caused her emotions to spiral out of control.

Her thoughts became shaped in a way that caused her suspicions to turn into a threat, which in turn caused a fight-or-flight response by putting on her jacket and shoes and leaving the safety of her house. Which in turn added worry and stress to her daughters who were concerned about her welfare.

## Can You Experience Stress and Anxiety at the Same Time?

In addition to anxiety, fear and stress are the biggest contributors to loss of emotional control.

**Fear...**

- is the feeling that something bad might happen, when in reality it seldom, if ever, does.

- does not necessarily mean being frightened of people, surroundings or events. But it can be brought on by insecurity, self-doubt and constant worries that are beyond one's control.

- can be the experience attached to the object of distress. For instance, a person who's had a bad bicycling or motorcycle accident might become nervous or anxious every time they see a bicycle or motorcycle. Or a person who was ridiculed in public, or in front of a peer group, might become fearful while in a social gathering.

**Stress...**

No one can escape stress in today's multitasking, demanding society.

Stress is a state of mental or emotional pressure or tension due to adverse or very demanding circumstances.

It's also defined as a response to internal or external stimuli that trigger a fight-or-flight response when the body reacts to certain stressors.

If left uncontrolled, stress can squeeze its hands around your neck and overpower you to the point you cease to function properly. But coping mechanisms, such as the ones I teach in this book, can control how quickly you respond to, then control, stress so it doesn't create even more stress.

## Can Anxiety Lead to Depression?

It's believed that anxiety can lead certain individuals to depression.

Dr. Aaron Beck (a pioneer of cognitive behavior therapy who developed many self-reporting measures to determine anxiety and depression, such as the Beck Depression Inventory or BDI) suggests that symptoms of anxiety and depression have a tendency to overlap. Whereas depression in its full expression moves away from anxiety.

A prolonged state of dissatisfaction, and mounting pressures such as constantly worrying about not finishing what you started, or unfulfilled daily goals, can make you feel frustrated, discouraged and unhappy.

Of course, it's unrealistic to expect you could escape anxiety or feeling overwhelmed altogether. For example, a particular event could temporarily cause deep emotional distress and anxiety.

However, if gone unchecked, anxiety can manifest hopelessness, despair and depression, which leads to thoughts of abandoning goals that could eventually lead to rewards... if you just hadn't given up and given in to your self-doubt.

It's critical to know that anxiety doesn't solve problems, nor will it help you live longer. Prolonged anxiety is more likely to shorten your life due to the negative effects it has on you psychologically and physiologically. For instance, you might find yourself feeling sad and discouraged, and lacking self-esteem. The future holds no hope because you feel as though you've lost control over your life. Whereas the reality is once you gain control over your emotions, you *can* feel happy, encouraged, and have self-esteem and hope for a wonderful, exciting future!

Over the centuries, many famous people realized they wasted a great deal of time worrying about things that caused them anxiety or depression. While reflecting back on his reign as Britain's Prime Minister during World War II, Sir Winston Churchill state, "When I look back on all these worries, I remember the story of the old man who said on his deathbed that he had had a lot of trouble in his life, most of which had never happened."

Mark Twain said, "I am an old man and have known a great many troubles, but most of them never happened."

Even Dale Carnegie, a famous American author and developer of self-improvement course, said to stop worrying and start living: "If you can't sleep, then get up and do something instead of lying there worrying. It's the worry that gets you, not the lack of sleep." (Carnegie, *How to Stop Worrying and Start Living*, 1944)

***Are you beginning to understand that anxiety doesn't have to control your life?***

## Controlling Stress and Anxiety One Step at a Time

When you were an infant, the knowledge you gained was most likely from a caregiver such as your parents. Regardless of whether it was right or wrong, it often resulted in positive or negative emotions, fears, expectations and/or anxieties you carried through to adulthood.

Everything was a fact, even if it was inaccurate, wrong, or told with a subversive purpose, and undoubtedly created a great impression in your little mind.

### Bombarded by Media Attacks and Subliminal Brainwashing

When you became an adult, watching news or reading articles written by someone who hasn't thought about the consequences can lead to misunderstanding, and misconceptions.

Misinformation can make a deep impression on a reader who's susceptible to inadvertent brainwashing.

Today, people are constantly inundated with ads and social media that push them to multitask. They talk on the phone while getting ready for work, cooking, eating, helping their kids with homework, or even while watching television.

Even worse, they'll shave or eat while driving because they haven't properly managed their time.

Today's complicated hustle-bustle world pushes people to become overwhelmed, unfeeling robots. They work through an entire day without taking breaks to de-stress, which produces additional hormones and chemicals that create uneasy feelings.

Because they don't understand what's happening to their body, their stress can become unmanageable and out of control.

(Even while you're reading this, you might be wondering how you'll find the time to complete work deadlines, pay the bills, run errands, take your kids to soccer or to doctor's appointments, write letters, or wash the clothes piling up in the laundry room. There's no time for yourself as it's whittled away by the constant demands placed on you.)

Breaking chores and responsibilities into smaller, more manageable tasks (that I discuss in a later chapter) prevents overlapping of bodily responses. Attacking them one at a time removes stress, and adds enjoyment to the process.

Creating a daily task calendar helps your mind to become organized. Little by little you'll discover that taking control of your actions will elevate the quality of your life to another level.

One action under control cascading into more actions under control is the key to opening the door to awareness, self-control, and taking charge of your life.

***How you approach your everyday tasks will help you become skilled in avoiding stress.***

## *Exercise 3: Finding Harmony During Your Day*

Identifying what causes stress, then finding ways to reduce or eliminate it, can create a more harmonic sense of well-being at home and at work.

In this exercise you'll write down one or more uncomfortable situations that cause you stress (i.e., being in a social meeting, running into a stranger, being angry at someone, running, etc.):

_______________________________________________

_______________________________________________

_______________________________________________

_______________________________________________

_______________________________________________

Based on what you've learned so far, how do you think you can monitor your thoughts, emotions and behaviors in situations that trigger negative feelings before you enter these situations? For example, if you have a situation that causes you to recall an unpleasant emotion (sadness, anger, anxiousness, fear, worry, etc.).

Develop a positive coping strategy requires having specific, constructive and clear thoughts and images (visualization), which will require you to believe in your alternative responses.

You'll need to do this exercise every day while changing unproductive behaviors to productive ones. Replacing outdated mindsets with new thoughts, emotions and actions such as determination, encouragement, hope and contentment will then create "the new you" you're longing to be.

Although it might feel a bit taxing to do this exercise every day during the process of changing old crippling behaviors to new productive ones, I want you to feel assured that each outcome will be better every time you utilize these tools.

# Chapter Five

## *UNDER THE UMBRELLA OF ANXIETY DISORDERS*

**"The perfect is the enemy of the good."**
**~Voltaire, French historian and author**

Mental illness or psychological disorders can be challenging to diagnose since they can take many forms.

For example, a person might experience both a generalized anxiety disorder and a bipolar and panic disorder at the same time. Yet, one or more of those conditions could remain undiagnosed as they can be difficult to recognize.

## Determining Your Specific Anxiety Disorder

Though all the disorders I discuss have anxiety at their core, they differ in the types of objects or situations that provoke fear or avoidance based on the content of a person's thoughts or beliefs.

Therefore, it's important to become familiar with what anxiety does in your mind and body.

For example, if you have a generalized anxiety disorder, you might be a persistent worrier. Your muscles – especially those in your face and shoulders – tighten, and you're in a constant state of heightened awareness.

Or if you have social anxiety, you're preoccupied with what other people might think about you.

***Are you following me so far?***

In general, an anxious individual has a negative appraisal of themselves or others, as well as the way they perceive the world.

Eventually those negative assessments will lead to lowered self-appreciation and self-confidence (seeing the dark side versus the bright side, or good versus evil. You know, that old notion of a glass half-full, half-empty.)

Thus, you can achieve a reasonable balance by maintaining awareness of your condition, which prevents your thoughts from spinning out of control over *perceived* negative evaluations.

## Bringing Your Disorder Up-to-Date

The difference between an anxiety disorder, versus an OCD or trauma and stressor-related disorder, is that an anxious person lives in a constant state of worry that's difficult to control because the disorder itself is caused by the mind.

Whereas trauma, stressors and obsessions create tension associated with an external factor (i.e., a loved one's serious illness, being overwhelmed by everyday routines, a troubled marriage, the stress of moving, etc.).

Treatments have thankfully come a long way from the horrific use of electroshock therapy, water and ice immersion tanks, induced malarial infections, and even lobotomies to treat even the simplest forms of anxiety disorders, panic attacks and depression:

> *"In the 1940s and 1950s, chemists began to experiment with different powders and pills that could calm imbalances inside the brain and deliver real relief to people who had mental illnesses. Rather than strapping people down to their beds, or asking people to simply talk about their problems, these chemists hoped to use a form of chemical restraint. People would feel better, and they might behave better, and no institutionalization would be needed at all."* (DualDiagnosis.org)

Per the new edition of the *Diagnostic Manual of Mental Disorders 5*, some of the categories for anxiety disorders have changed, while much has remained the same for anxiety and depression.

Some disorders are now in three definitive categories:

1) Anxiety Disorders; 2) Obsessive-Compulsive and Related Disorders; and 3) Trauma-and Stressor-Related Disorders. This change emphasizes the distinctiveness of each category, while having anxiety as the common denominator.

The following chart should help clarify the different kinds of anxiety disorders to help you realize that what you're experiencing doesn't fall under these categories. Or to help you find the right therapist and treatment(s) for your particular disorder.

*NOTE: Please remember that self-diagnosing can be dangerous, especially if it's the wrong condition. If you're worried that you might be suffering from anxiety, or any of these disorders, please consult a specialist who can guide you to the correct treatment protocol.*

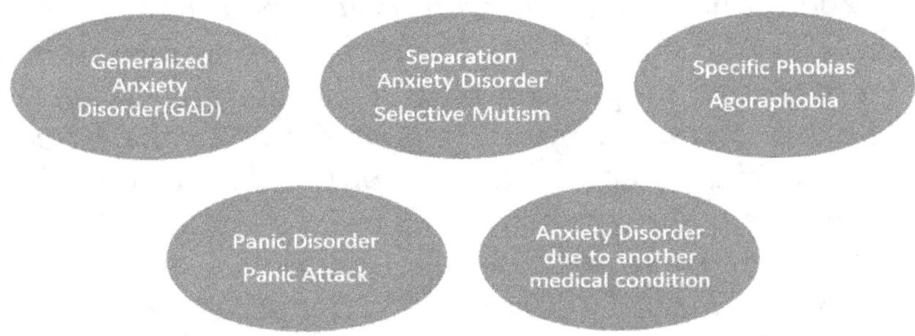


## *Generalized Anxiety Disorder (GAD)*

- An individual experiences excessive worry and anxiety about common everyday activities for a period of at least six months.

- They find it difficult to control their worrying.

- Their anxieties and worries are associated with at least three of these symptoms: restlessness or feeling keyed up; easily fatigued; difficulty concentrating, or their mind goes blank; irritability; tight muscles; or sleep disturbance(s) such as insomnia.

- Their worry or anxiety causes impairment of social, occupational, or other areas of functioning.

- Their anxiety isn't the result of direct use of drug abuse, medication, or a general medical condition.

To illustrate, while at work a person with GAD worries about their job responsibilities. At home they worry about chores, appointments, family health, car repairs, or children being late to school. They might have problems sleeping because they continually ruminate on everything in their life.

They might constantly complain of muscle aches and tension (one of the most common symptoms), feeling shaky, weak, and/or light-headed. They can become irritable and exhausted, and lack concentration and the ability to work efficiently due to their constant worrying.

## *Phobic Disorders*

- Specific Phobia: An exaggerated, unreasonable fear shown by the presence of a particular object or situation, such as animals or insects, natural environments, storms, blood injection injury, closed spaces, or other situations.

- Social Phobia (aka: Social Anxiety Disorder or SAD): A persistent fear of being exposed to scrutiny while in social situations, speaking or eating in public, or during a conversation.

SAD is the cognitive ideation (the process to create a thought) of being negatively evaluated by or offending others, or by being embarrassed, humiliated or rejected. Their fear, anxiety or avoidance is out of proportion to the real threat posed by the social circumstance, and to the sociocultural context.

For instance, if you experience social anxiety, you might worry excessively and fear what people might think of you. If they disagree with you, you're worried could say something that might offend someone or embarrass you. You'd also be concerned about interacting with others, including family members, friends or neighbors.

At work you'd worry about being negatively evaluated when interacting with authority figures, or when giving presentations during meetings. You worry whenever someone calls because you think you did something wrong (self-negative evaluations). Then later you realize you blew their intentions completely out of proportion.

### *Panic Disorder*

A panic attack is an abrupt surge of intense fear or discomfort that quickly peaks. Escalating from a calm to an anxious state, it's characterized by four or more of the following symptoms:

- accelerated heart palpitations
- sweating
- trembling
- shortness of breath
- choking feeling, like hands are around your throat

- nausea
- lightheadedness or fainting
- fear of dying, losing control, or "going crazy"
- tingling sensations in extremities
- feelings of being detached from oneself
- dismay, anxiety and confusion
- persistently concerned or worried about additional panic attacks or their consequences (i.e., losing control, having a heart attack, or "going over the edge")

## Obsessive-Compulsive Disorder (OCD)

In the movie, *As Good As it Gets*, Melvin Udall (Jack Nicholson) had severe OCD where he *had* to open and close the door lock four times, turn lights on and off five times, furiously scrub his hands with hot water while using a bar of soap only once, use his own utensils in a restaurant, and was terrified of stepping on a sidewalk crack.

Though this is an extreme example, this kind of severe behavior does exist. An Obsessive-Compulsive Disorder can cripple a person to the point they cease to function in any kind of environment.

## OCD Versus OCPD

It's important to know the difference between OCD and Obsessive-Compulsive Personality Disorder (OCPD) as they're completely different, and therefore need to be treated differently.

OCD is an anxiety disorder. Obsessions are characterized by intrusive, distressful and inappropriate images or thoughts.

These thoughts or images aren't just about real life problems, but imagined events or situations. Therefore, OCD might be present with either obsessions or compulsions, or both, the latter of which is the most common presentation.

Whereas OCPD is a personality disorder. According to the definition at Healthline.com:

*"Obsessive compulsive personality disorder (OCPD) is a personality disorder that's characterized by extreme perfectionism, order, and neatness. People with OCPD will also feel a severe need to impose their own standards on their outside environment. People with OCPD have the following characteristics:*

- *They find it hard to express their feelings.*
- *They have difficulty forming and maintaining close relationships with others.*
- *They're hard-working. But their obsession with perfection can make them inefficient.*
- *They often feel righteous, indignant, and angry.*
- *They often face social isolation.*
- *They can experience anxiety that occurs with depression.*

*OCPD is often confused with an anxiety disorder called obsessive-compulsive disorder (OCD).*

*However, they aren't the same. People with OCPD have no idea there's anything wrong with the way they think or behave. They believe their way of thinking and doing things is the only correct way and that everyone else is wrong."* (Watson, 2015)

Regardless of which of the two disorders a person might have, obsessions or compulsions are time-consuming and interrupt daily functioning.

For instance, when taking a shower they must always follow the same steps in the same sequence. If they miss one step, they'll start over until they're satisfied they've precisely followed each and every step.

For obvious reasons, for these kinds of individuals taking a shower can take a very long time.

The actions a person with OCD or OCPD take provide only temporary relief from their anxiety. However, with early diagnosis and the right therapy, the suffering that comes with their disorder can be avoided.

### *Post-Traumatic Stress Disorder (PTSD)*

Although PTSD often surfaces in the media related to war veterans due to physical, psychological and emotional trauma, it's been around for hundreds of years with different names:  Shell shock, battle fatigue, Soldier's Heart, Railway Spine, and nostalgia which was first coined by Austrian physician Josef Leopold in 1761.

According to the University of Maryland Medical Center, PTSD (which is no longer considered an anxiety disorder In the DSM-5 "Diagnostic and Statistical Manual of Mental Disorders" 5th ed.) is brought on by recurrent memories of extremely stressful events a person experienced or witnessed:

*"More than 5 million adults in the United States are affected by PTSD each year. Symptoms of PTSD usually develop within the first 3 months after the event, but they may not surface until months or even years after the original traumatic event. Symptoms may include:*

- *Recurrent, involuntary and intrusive thoughts recalling the traumatic event [children might express this symptom in repetitive play]*
- *Nightmares [children might have disturbing dreams without the content being related to trauma]*
- *Flashbacks [children might reenact the event while playing]*
- *Efforts to avoid feelings and thoughts that either remind [the person] of the traumatic event or that trigger similar feelings*
- *Feeling detached or unable to connect with loved ones*
- *Depression, hopelessness*
- *Feelings of guilt (from the false belief that [the person] is responsible for the traumatic incident)*
- *Irritability or angry outbursts*
- *Hyper-vigilance (being overly aware of possible danger)*
- *Hypersensitivity, including at least two of the following reactions: trouble sleeping, being angry, having difficulty concentrating, startling easily, having a physical reaction (rapid heart rate or breathing, increase in blood pressure)*
- *Headache*
- *Disrupted sleep, insomnia."* (Post-Traumatic Stress Disorder, UMMC)

Individuals displaying symptoms of PTSD often...

- have a history of sexual or physical abuse.
- work in a high-risk civil service occupation, such as firefighting, the military, or law enforcement.
- have a history of depression or other psychological disorder(s).
- abuse drugs or alcohol.
- don't have an adequate support system.
- survived traumatic events such as car wrecks, fires, terrorist attacks, or natural disasters.
- are depressed and anxious.

(It's interesting to note that women are twice as likely as men to show signs of PTSD.)

## CASE STUDY THREE:  CHARLIE

After Charlie was diagnosed with clinical depression, he was hospitalized for two excruciating long weeks. Experiencing turbulent times as a teenager facing uncertainty and scrutiny played a part in his diagnosis.

According to my assessment, Charlie should have been classified as experiencing episodic depression rather than being labeled with clinical depression. To me, his main problem was a generalized anxiety disorder, which, according to some sources such as Dr. Aaron Beck, in some cases can lead to any type of depression.

The psychiatrist at the hospital prescribed antidepressants, which he took for one month. Instead of feeling healthier, he became even more depressed and chose to stop taking the medication.

The question about Charlie's type of depression was finally resolved about six months later.

Once psychotherapy helped identify the cause of Charlie's anxiety and sleep disturbances, our team was able to control his moods and work on his emotional attachments.

I'm not saying that a person with an emotional deep disturbance is healed after only twelve therapy sessions. But Charlie was ready to move on because he knew he could maintain a better level of functionality by asking for help.

I'm pleased to report that Charlie's had a stable job for several years. He's reliable and no longer calls in sick. He's responsibly performing tasks at his job and in his therapy sessions because he learned how to optimally use the "psychological tools" he was taught.

Of course, like anyone Charlie will have down days. But if he continues his treatment protocol, I'm confident he'll successfully manage his life.

*With preparation, hard work and determination there are no limits to positively controlling emotional and mental distress.*

## Trauma-Related Disorders and Stressors

Frequently, a person's reaction is initially known as *acute stress disorder* in the immediate aftermath of some sort of trauma. In approximately one-half of adults, the symptoms might disappear within as little as three months.

Whereas in the other half, the symptoms could remain for up to twelve months, and much longer in a small percentage of people.

Although trauma-related disorders and stressors (including PTSD) have been classified in a distinctive category from anxiety disorders, they still have anxiety as a common denominator:

### *Stressor...*

- An individual, or a family member or close friend, experiences a traumatic event that's perceived as a physical, harmful threat, or one that could potentially cause death.

- Children six years and younger learn a traumatic event(s) occurred to a parent or caregiver.

- Recurrent, involuntary, and intrusive distressing memories of one or more traumatic events.

During and/or after the event, a person presents at least three of the following dissociative symptoms:

1. emotional numbing
2. detachment or no emotional response
3. decrease in awareness of their surroundings
4. de-realization (a feeling that one's surroundings aren't real, especially as a symptom of mental disturbance)
5. depersonalization (regarding one's mind or body, can consist of a detachment within the self, or being a detached observer of one's self)
6. the inability to recall important aspects of the trauma

### *The traumatic event...*

- *is re-experienced* as a flashback of images, thoughts, and dreams. Intense psychological distress, or marked avoidance of the stimuli, causes memories of the traumatic event to constantly resurface.

- *creates avoidance* of thoughts, feelings or conversations associated with the trauma. The individual tries to avoid places, people or activities that remind them of the trauma.

- *exacerbates arousal.* The individual experiences increased stimuli such as poor concentration, irritability, or exaggerated startle responses. Irritable behavior and angry outbursts, with little or no provocation, are typically expressed as verbal or physical aggression towards people or objects.

- *causes significant impairment* in social, occupational or other important areas of functioning.

The disturbances can last longer than one month.

To illustrate, an individual suffering from trauma-related disorders and stressors must have been exposed to one or more traumatic events. (To clarify, a life-threatening illness or debilitating medical condition isn't necessarily considered a traumatic event.) A person can constantly have involuntary, intrusive recollections of a shocking event. Whereas in other instances they might present themselves with dissociative states that last from a few seconds to several hours.

During this state, the individual feels as if the event was occurring right at that moment. They disconnect from their reality, and absorb the personality of who they perceived they were during the trauma.

Since anxiety exists because of *perceived* fear, instead of reality, you can change your mindset to see the situation as non-threatening, dangerous or destructive.

For example, you could ask yourself, *what kind of evidence is there to prove that this fear or threat is real? What's the worst that could happen to me? What could be the outcome of changing my thinking?*

## Exercise 4: CBT for Dysfunctional Thought Record

"CBT" stands for Cognitive Behavior Therapy.

Whenever you notice your mood changing, ask yourself what's going through your mind at that very moment. Then immediately write down the thought or image so you can capture it, then review it to understand what's causing this particular change in your mood.

The situation (describe the event leading to the unpleasant emotion. Or the stream of thoughts or recollection leading to the unpleasant emotion.):

_______________________________________________

_______________________________________________

_______________________________________________

_______________________________________________

_______________________________________________

List any negative automatic thoughts that preceded the emotion. Then rate your belief about those thoughts on a scale from 1 to 10 (1 being you don't believe them, up to 10 where you fully believe them) so you can track the progress and intensity of your beliefs and your emotions.

____________________________________

____________________________________

____________________________________

____________________________________

____________________________________

Rating: _____

What were your emotion(s) when you experienced the mood change (were you sad, angry, anxious, frustrated, etc.?):

____________________________________

____________________________________

____________________________________

____________________________________

____________________________________

List any cognitive distortions that altered your mood to create a "mountain out of a mole hill" situation (also called "catastrophizing").

For example, all-or-nothing thinking; over-generalization; eliminating the positive while focusing on the negative; jumping to conclusions; magnifying or minimizing your emotions; emotional reasoning; 'should statements' [I should be this, I should do that, etc.]; labeling or mislabeling:

---
---
---
---
---

Think about an alternative, more rational response you could have had to your mood change. Then rate your belief about your response from 1 to 10 (1 being you don't believe it, up to 10 where you fully believe it):

---
---
---
---
---

Rating: _____

You – and only you – can choose whether to have positive or negative viewpoints of the world so you can experience joy, calmness, and inner peace.

**Now it's time to take charge of your life!**

# Chapter Six

## *TAKING CHARGE OF YOUR LIFE!*

**"The person faithful in what is least
is faithful also in much,
and the person unrighteous in what is least
is unrighteous also in much."
~Luke 16:10 (New World Translation of the Holy
Scriptures)**

This wise proverb means that if you do one thing well, you can do other things at the same level of competency. Likewise, bad habits can control many areas of your life unless you eliminate them.

While I was at university, I began a friendship with a fellow student. At first we chatted here and there, then we started studying together. The more we got to know each other better, she began to display inconsiderate conduct like not returning a jacket or repaying money I loaned her.

But I chose to ignore those annoyances because they were insignificant compared to our friendship. After a few years, her complete disregard for people's feelings became even more evident. When she didn't offer to repair a dent she had put in a friend's car, I wondered how many other aspects of her life had been affected by her negative, narcissistic behavior.

Applying the principle that if a person is unrighteous to others they are unrighteous to themselves, not only was she in debt to her friends, but in debt with herself because she hadn't finished enough courses to graduate with me.

Now let's flip that situation to a positive one. Having one event under control means you can control other events. While the event itself isn't the controlling factor, the skills you acquire while gaining control over your actions, feelings and thoughts are.

Being in control means taking *charge of your life* because you're stronger, wiser, and more powerful than your emotions!

## Regulating Your Emotions, Feelings and Actions

Thus far you've learned that fear is a result of a negative or pessimistic outlook on life. Anxiety is fear causing your emotions to race out of control. And stress is your body's physiological reaction to external events and situations.

***Now that you know how to differentiate your thoughts from your fears, you can begin to regulate your feelings and actions.***

The following might feel like the converse to what I'm discussing. But it's okay to feel some stress because it shows that you're concerned about your life, that you appreciate the people in your life, and that you're searching for better solutions.

Besides, you're only human, and negative emotions can rear their ugly head at any time. How you prevent them from getting out of control is the crucial factor.

The kind of overpowering, debilitating stress I'm discussing can destroy your life, relationships and goals. So you can either allow it to control you, or you can control it.

**Your path is yours to choose.**

## Knowing When to Ask for and Accept Help

Because today's society is more open to discussing psychological issues such as anxiety disorders, there are many treatments and research that weren't available even ten years ago.

Realizing a healthy mind and body means a healthy lifestyle, going to a therapist is more commonplace in the States where issues are discussed more openly. Knowing the right moment to seek help depends on an individual's particular situation.

Some people realize they need professional help and consult a therapist. While some are too embarrassed to reach out, or think their problems will disappear.

There's no one-size-fits all panacea for getting anxiety and panic under control as everyone's issues causing them are different.

If you're not quite ready to ask for help, or don't know what might be causing your problems, hopefully my book will prove that there are many ways to address anxiety disorders beyond antiquated methods of treatment.

## Knowing When to Get Professional Assistance

Because many people believe that mental disorders can lead to instability, conflict and emotional turbulence, they balk at seeking treatment because they feel ashamed, or have previously experienced a lack of compassion for their situation.

Some people seek help right away, whereas others will wait years or never seek help. I've found that most people finally seek professional assistance when their symptoms become unbearable, or greatly interfere with their work, home life and relationships.

As a therapist, my first step is to make my clients feel comfortable and relaxed, as though they were stretched out on a comfy couch where they can freely and safely express their concerns.

My office is a safe haven, a sanctuary if you will, where they become the leaders of their choices without any judgment or criticism as that's not my role as a therapist.

I validate their feelings by carefully listening to and taking their feelings seriously (the kind of encouragement they've lacked from people who should be their biggest supporters like friends, spouses and loved ones.)

Transference (or transference neurosis during therapy sessions) means a therapist feels emotions from the person's childhood, or any other time in their life that causes anxiety, uncontrolled emotions, or panic attacks to be triggered.

Unlike other therapists, I prefer not to give advice to my clients as it's up to them to figure out their problems based on the work I do with them. However, some transference is necessary to show them that I trust they're completely capable of coming up with their own conclusions during our therapy sessions.

You might think generic questions like "What brought you here?" and "Tell me how you feel" are too broad-based. But they're the types of questions that create a comfortable symbiosis between patient and therapist as the patient feels their thoughts, feelings and emotions are being validated, supported and understood.

## CASE STUDY FOUR: JANE

Even though Jane was suspicious, hesitant, reserved and anxious when she first came to my office, she didn't hesitate to discuss her medical problems, which helped me create a psychological and experiential background profile for her issues.

In spite of her behavior, she was highly motivated to become well, and cooperated fully by completing all the assignments I gave her.

By our eleventh session she said she felt she no longer needed therapy, and was ready to begin living a new life. A few months after our last session I learned that she ended a deteriorating seventeen-year relationship (which I found interesting as it had only been discussed once).

During her sessions I helped her build the foundation on which to reorganize her emotions, determine her feelings, and what behaviors to change. Because she'd been a willing participant, she implemented the principles I taught her into making wise decisions and taking decisive actions once her sessions were done.

As a psychotherapist it was very refreshing to work with a client who instinctively knew when she was ready to begin therapy, and when to get on with her life. Since my style of therapy is typically short-term, I inform my clients that the focus of their treatment will be learning how to use basic tools they can use for the rest of their lives.

Jane learned the tools, techniques and strategies I taught her, and now happily lives alone with her two daughters.

## CASE STUDY FIVE:  ROBERT

Robert had achieved a successful career during his early forties, but was struggling to find his purpose in a highly competitive business world. Though he'd made goals since his early twenties, not one had been actualized because he stopped thinking about them once he found a well-paying job.

At first he had fun traveling and purchasing many material items. He didn't think he needed a "to-do list" (or bucket list as it's often called) as his plans could wait. Or worse, they no longer mattered. The more he got caught up in the whirlwind of success, the more his original plans became faded memories.

One day Robert ran into a friend with whom he'd shared life goals when they were young men. His friend telling him he'd actually accomplished his plans, and that he was living a rewarding life, triggered a terrible ache and longing in Robert's heart for the life he hadn't actualized.

After their meeting, no one noticed he'd become depressed because he kept his thoughts to himself.

But at the end of each day, he still had to face the reality that he no longer wanted the life he was living. He felt like a disappointment and a failure because nothing on his bucket list had been checked off.

During our sessions I had him write down the dreams and goals he felt were achievable, and the timeframe in which they could be achieved.

We also worked on changing his behaviors by starting to be less social so he could stay focused on his goals (noting that people need to achieve a proper work/life balance to achieve goals at work and in their personal life).

Once I had him create a "want to-do list" versus a "must-do" list, he immediately started working on his plans since each session, at least in the beginning, would strictly focus on actualizing his goals.

At the end of his short-term therapy, Robert felt more comfortable saying no to his friends when they asked him to socialize.

Because he felt happier, he turned his focus to having a career that would be satisfying, fulfilling, and what he truly wanted.

After a few follow-ups I never saw Robert again, so I hope he's now walking his chosen path.

## Exercise 5: CBT in Action to Work On Your Emotions

Again, CBT stands for Cognitive Behavior Therapy. Monitoring your thoughts and emotions in situations that trigger negative feelings helps you learn about your methods of thinking and behavior. Then over time the patterns will change based on your comprehension of why emotions manifest in certain ways.

Use this exercise to record any situations that trigger anxiety or low moods:

Analyze the situation and any triggers that might have caused it. (What happened? Where were you, and who were you with when it happened? Why do you think it happened?)

_______________________________________________

_______________________________________________

_______________________________________________

_______________________________________________

_______________________________________________

Write down any negative thoughts and/or emotions you had before, during and after the situation (What was going through your mind at the time? What one or more things did you find disturbing, such as the environment, people, sounds, etc.?)

_______________________________________________

_______________________________________________

_______________________________________________

_______________________________________________

_______________________________________________

What kinds of emotion(s) were you feeling? (On a scale from 1 to 10 – 1 being not severe, to 10 being severe – rate how the emotions felt.):

______________________________________________
______________________________________________
______________________________________________
______________________________________________
______________________________________________

Rating: ______

What kinds of physical sensations were you feeling? And where in your body did you feel them (stomach, head, neck, back, etc.)?

______________________________________________
______________________________________________
______________________________________________
______________________________________________
______________________________________________

Assessing your emotions and behavior can help you develop strategies to cope with negative and/or debilitating thoughts or emotions. After all, the point is to gain control of situations before they gain control of you!

# Chapter Seven

## *PREOCCUPATION VERSUS PROCRASTINATION*

**"My advice is never do tomorrow
what you can do today.
Procrastination is the thief of time. Collar him!"
~Charles Dickens, author of *David Copperfield***

## Understanding the Difference

People who are constantly worried can become preoccupied about what others might think about them. Because it's difficult to stay focused, they can become even more anxious while struggling to remember instructions they're given, or what they're supposed to be doing.

The good news is this isn't the result of a memory disorder, but rather preoccupation or the inability to pay attention.

In Vivian Leigh's famous scene at the end of the movie, *Gone With the Wind* (1939), Scarlett O'Hara is wondering how she'll get her beloved Rhett back into her arms. "I'll think of some way to get him back. After all, tomorrow is another day."

Whereas procrastination is a major contributing factor of anxiety. It's the "later" or "in a little while" or "I'll do it tomorrow" people use as an excuse for not wanting to do something.

Confronting a difficult task is tough enough, so why add to your anxiety by putting off what you'll eventually have to do?

You set the alarm for 7:00 a.m., then keep hitting the snooze button. Later you're exhausted after your day's work, so you put off making calls for the next day.

Or you have housework or laundry that needs to be done. But you put off doing it until the next day (or the next... or the next) because you're just too overwhelmed by all your responsibilities.

The more you put things off, the more things pile up... and the more stress you experience. And so the ugly cycle of procrastination continues.

## CASE STUDY SIX: TIMOTHY

Timothy was constantly avoiding responsibilities, which caused many problems in his daily life. He was a typical procrastinator who found excuses not to do things from the moment he woke up throughout the rest of his day.

During his sessions Timothy talked about his past experiences while trying to look for the root cause of his issues of procrastination. He learned that past events, like the life his parents felt he should live versus the one he should really live, prevented him from emotional growth and being able to eventually have his own family.

Because he didn't know how to effectively and assertively communicate with his parents, his goals and dreams suffered.

Instead of reaching beyond his capabilities, he created a pattern of procrastination to prevent failure, being hurt, abandoned and/or rejected.

Behavioral therapy focuses treatment on a person's cognitive process. I could have spent countless years trying to help Timothy to ferret out what had happened in his past to cause his patterns of procrastination.

But working with real-time processes made him realize that the techniques I was teaching him to manage his life was the critical factor in his wellness plan.

Patterns of self-adjustments or excuses are characteristic of procrastination. They can provide comfort but not good outcomes.

Whereas, patterns of discipline and action will produce good results and comfort.

During his sessions, Timothy was surprised to learn his mind had been subconsciously tricking him into acting in repetitive patterns.

Once he realized the past shouldn't determine how he should be living in the present, Timothy no longer procrastinated and became fully invested in his life.

## Breaking Your Daily To-Do List into Manageable Tasks

*"Thirty years ago my older brother, who was ten years old at the time, was trying to get a report written on birds that he'd had three months to write, which was due the next day.*
*We were out at our family cabin in Bolinas, and he was at the kitchen table close to tears, surrounded by binder paper and pencils and unopened books about birds, immobilized by the hugeness of the task ahead. Then my father sat down beside him put his arm around my brother's shoulder, and said, "Bird by bird, buddy. Just take it bird by bird."*
~**Anne Lamott**, author of *Bird by Bird*

An effective way to tackle your to-do list and avoid procrastination is to break big tasks into manageable sizes. Or as the above quote says, "bird by bird."

Even though Ms. Lamott's quote applies to writing, it can apply to anything you're trying to accomplish.

By checking tasks off your list one at a time, before you know it you'll have completed your entire daily, weekly, monthly and yearly to-do lists!

Not organizing and prioritizing routine tasks can cause them to become burdensome, stressful and frustrating.

The good news is time management is as simple as first identifying activities you'll be doing on a daily basis, then allotting the approximate time you'll need to do them:

1. Write a daily to-do list. Then sync your calendar with your computer, cell phone, or any other electronic devices you use. Or handwrite tasks in a notebook you can carry with you.

2. Write an action plan by setting realistic priorities. Writing down the steps it will take to accomplish your goals can eliminate stress and anxiety, especially if you combine several steps into one (i.e., on your way to your child's school you can pick up the dry cleaning, drop off books at the library, and pick up dog food at the pet store).

3. Schedule less and don't overload your agenda. Speaking from experience, I know this can be difficult for busy parents to do. But quite often there are tasks that can either be set aside for moments when there's spare time, such as mothers trying to balance a family, or eliminate them altogether if they're not really important.

   Writing down timeframes doesn't mean you're bound to them as they're a goal to shoot for. But like the 80:20 Pareto principle states, 80% of results are obtained with 20% of effort. Therefore, you should try to complete at least 80% of the things on your list to eliminate stress and give you a sense of accomplishment.

4. Avoid interruptions. Tell yourself you're going to focus on a task, then immediately start doing it.

5. Take periodic breaks. Creating moments of recreation for you and your family, plus setting time aside for yourself for "de-stressing," is critical for your mental health and well-being.

6. Start managing your time right away. The sooner you gain control over your time, the sooner you can enjoy your life to its fullest!

## *Exercise 6: Tips for Better Time Management*

The following calendaring exercise will show you how to first identify your *permanent values* such as family, health, friends, spirituality and work. Then the *not permanent values* that get checked off your list once they're achieved.

During a two-week period I'd like you to write down all the occurrences that sideswiped your plans, or took a lot of your time, which will help identify places in your agenda that need better time management.

The purpose of this following example is to plan a routine you can adjust whenever necessary. Organizing your time will help you to stay calm and focused, which in turn makes you happier because you've had a well-organized, productive day.

Many people tend to shy away from routines, but I've found that not having a routine can allow a day to get out of control. Also, not taking their life seriously by planning and enforcing those plans can make people lazy and boring.

Therefore, I assure you that time management allows you to improvise, be flexible and creative, and have more time for yourself (the latter of which should make you very excited!).

**6:00 a.m. to 8:00 a.m.: Begin your day**

- Get out of bed. Do your morning ablutions (i.e., take a shower, etc.)

- Review your to-do list for the day.

- Begin your daily routine (i.e., prepare breakfast, read the Bible, meditate, exercise, etc.).

- Get your children ready for school (bagged lunches, backpacks, homework, etc.). Optimally, getting the children ready should be shared by both parents to eliminate stress.

- Get dressed. Double-check everything you need (i.e., car keys, cell phone, briefcase, tote bag, etc.).

- Leave for work. Don't multitask while driving as it can be very dangerous as your attention is elsewhere. Listening to audiobooks can help a commute be relaxing and entertaining while maintaining your focus on the road ahead of you.

**9:00 a.m.: Start your workday (the same applies whether you go to an office or stay at home).**

Getting to your office at least ten minutes early to de-stress prepares your mind for whatever arises during the day.

Or if you're at home, meditating, doing exercises, or just sitting on your patio with a cup of coffee or tea for ten minutes prepares you for your day.

## 12:00 p.m. to 1:00 p.m.: Lunchtime

Take at least 30 minutes to eat a healthy lunch. If you have another 30 minutes, do something else like walking or reading.

Taking time for yourself will help you function better as you'll have a willing heart and rested mind.

## 1:00 p.m.: Back to work (or running errands if you don't go to an office)

If you're not relaxed after having a restful lunch, think about what might be bothering you.

Is a situation at work making you unhappy? Did you have an argument with a co-worker, or your spouse before you went to work? Try to come up with a solution so you don't carry your emotions back home with you.

And don't procrastinate! Working through things now will make you a happy "professional" in both your work/home life.

## 5:00 p.m.: Return home

While staying focused on your driving, visualize your house as a safe haven to come home to. During drive time, repeat positive affirmations such as *I'm aware of the kinds of negative thoughts I fabricate in my mind. I can have positive thoughts and bring good things into my life.*

Remember, the same effort is required for your mind to have negative or positive thoughts. Being the master of your inner peace is your contribution to your and your family's well-being.

***You can choose to either be happy or sad, so why not be happy!***

**5:00 p.m. to 10:00 p.m.: Dinner and the rest of your day**

If you have a family, it's very important to devote time to cooking then eating together, doing homework, playing games, and maybe even reading bedtime stories together. Spend quality time with your spouse so you both go to bed feeling well-loved and respected. (The same kind of quality time can be spent on yourself if you live alone!)

**10:00 p.m.: Time for bed**

Doing a few minutes of light exercise like bending and stretching, or reading a book, helps your body and mind to relax. Make sure the television and cell phones are off as you don't want anything to interrupt your sleep.

If you have children, enforce boundaries about coming into your bedroom as this is your time to de-stress and have adult time with your spouse.

Say positive affirmations about the tasks you completed, the wonderful time you had with your family, and what you'd like for the next day to put you into the proper mindset to be happy, healthy and content!

All of this preparation time creates a well-balanced space for you to bound into the next morning when you wake up!

# Chapter Eight

## *FINDING THE RIGHT SOLUTIONS*

*"Patience... is an expression of love for others.
It is closely connected with endurance,
which enable us to put up
with difficult circumstances while maintaining
a positive attitude."
~The Watchtower magazine (August, 2017)*

## Assessment, Commitment, Determination and Strategizing

No problem can be solved without first identifying it, then remaining steadfast to finding a solution to solve it. Making an honest, diligent effort to work on your problems will help you discover the path to a calmer, more peaceful life.

As an example, if you have difficulty controlling your emotions, you might have a tendency to react to people and situations with irritation, anger, frustration and defensiveness without considering the consequences of not filtering your words and/or behavior.

Over time you realize this is a significant obstacle preventing you from becoming a better person.

So finding a positive approach to incorporating carefully planned strategies into your daily routine is a perfect first step toward achieving inner balance.

## The Six Stages of Changing Behavior

These stages apply to any problem when addressing lifestyle modification. In other words, you can use them to set you free from negative behavior while seeking to become a better person.

Once you identify which behavior(s) are causing problems, you can find a solution for tackling them. As you read through this list, think about which one or more stages fit your current state of mind:

1. *Pre-contemplation* means that even though your problem is obvious to others, you're not aware of it and its risks.

   For example, hurting your relationships with loved ones because of your negative behavior.

2. *Contemplation:* Although you're still doubtful that you have anxiety as a problem, you contemplate the possibility of acknowledging then facing it.

3. *Preparation:* In this stage you begin to define realistic options for changing your behavior by identifying weaknesses, and exploring risky situations that might cause anxiety. You also develop strategies to prevent relapses.

4. *Action:* In this fourth stage you commit to invest time and energy to make lifestyle changes. You praise yourself whenever you successfully solve the problem. For example, you focus on progress rather than perfection.

   Reaffirm your decision as you contemplate small successes and continue to take decisive action. Positive results strengthen your conviction and determination to overcome obstacles.

5. *Maintenance:* While new behavior is being created, during this stage you might have difficulty staying motivated, and will be alert to high-risk situations that could lead to regression. However, once you become open to discussing your progress, you might also find opportunities to mentor others who are beginning the process of overcoming their anxiety.

6. *Relapse:* In the event of a setback, it's important to have a support system such as trusted friends, family members, or a therapist that can help you realize it's only temporary and you can re-engage in the change process. In the event you keep experiencing anxiety attacks that create havoc on your life, you need to understand the symptomology in order to regain control over your emotions, while remembering change is a process that doesn't occur overnight.

For example, you might encounter a situation where fear controls your thoughts, and anxiety escalates to a potential crisis. The first step is to recognize what's causing your fear, then take steps to rationalize and overcome it. Even though you might have minor setbacks, you're continuing the process of controlling your fears before they conquer you.

Realizing that anyone can experience these six stages of discovery can be the impetus for taking steps to have a better quality of life. Despite any obstacles and/or anxiety you're confronted with, giving yourself small rewards (even something as simple as going to a movie, eating an ice cream cone, buying a favorite magazine, going to a favorite restaurant, etc.) with each achievement makes life more pleasant and meaningful.

***Give it a try. After all, you have nothing to lose and a great deal to gain!***

## *Exercise 7: Ten Questions to Determine Your Level of Anxiety*

The following exercise is easy to do, and extremely liberating.

Grab a pen and paper, or an electronic device such as a notepad, you can take notes on. Then list ten questions you'd ask yourself while experiencing anxiety.

Write down the first thing that comes to your mind regardless of how crazy it sounds. (This will only take a few minutes, so keep writing until you finish all ten.)

Take a few moments to close your eyes, breathe deeply, and relax. Then open your eyes and look at your list. If something doesn't make sense, set it aside as random thoughts will eventually begin to take shape. If they don't, they're not important enough to make it onto your list.

Below are examples of the kinds of thoughts you might have:

- What am I thinking? And why am I thinking it?
- Does what I'm thinking make sense?
- Why is it difficult to write it down?
- How can I write it without anyone seeing it?
- Is what I'm thinking wrong?
- Do these kinds of thoughts sound crazy?
- Why is this happening to me?
- I don't understand any of these thoughts coursing through my mind.
- Am I afraid of something specific? Is it a place, an event, my job, my family, or even myself?
- Can I face these things? If not, what's preventing me from doing so?
- I have nothing to write.
- I'm writing what I'm thinking right now.
- I'm seeing more clearly now that I'm writing it down.
- I'm determined to do this exercise as often as necessary until I can define my anxiety, then tackle it head on.

Repeat this exercise often as new thoughts or recessed memories pop up all the time. Date each time you do this exercise so you can reflect back on earlier questions to keep track of your progress.

Did writing these down get easier? Did it help you to feel calmer? Were you able to determine what your anxiety or issues are, and how you might be able to overcome them? Did you figure out what triggers your anxiety or panic attacks?

Learning how to define then find solutions for your anxiety disorders takes time, so please be patient with yourself. Patterns can be changed, but only after they're recognized so you can devise a proper solution.

With that being said, the next chapter are some proven strategies and techniques to help you overcome your problems once they're identified.

# Chapter Nine

## *STRATEGIES AND TECHNIQUES FOR OVERCOMING ANXIETY*

*"Before you give up, remember:
You are almost there!
Difficulties increase the nearer
we approach the goal."*
**~Johann Wolfgang von Goethe**

## Is There a Cure for Anxiety?

Just like the hungry tiger above that's strategizing to catch its prey, you too can create strategies to overcome your problems.

By this point in the book, you should have begun to understand how your brain perceives situations as dangerous or threatening. There's always a common cognitive pattern to your thought processes.

Regardless of whether your perception is accurate or distorted, your thoughts can be your own. Or they can become skewed if they're based on how you think others perceive you.

The importance you place on each aspect of your life also influences how an event is observed, and how much positive or negative effect it has on you.

For example, your goal might be to go to a social gathering to find a companion. You dress and walk seductively to attract attention, whereas someone else dresses conservatively and exudes an air of professionalism. Each of you are projecting a particular image because you want to get something from the experience.

Or if you're at a business meeting, while someone is giving a presentation each attendee's experience will be radically different based on their observation and perception.

Studies have demonstrated a common denominator between individuals who have generalized anxiety disorder and social anxiety. While discussing their fears, they often apply the same thoughts and assumptions to the same situations.

To illustrate, "When people meet criteria for social anxiety disorder and another anxiety disorder, social anxiety comes first in 32% of people." (Chartier et al, 2003)

Following are common denominators that people with anxiety tend to exhibit:

- Any strange or uncomfortable situation is seen as dangerous or life-threatening.
- A situation or person isn't trustworthy until proven otherwise.
- It's safer to think about the worst-case scenario.

- Their safety is dependent on how well they're prepared for any possible dangerous situation.
- Their survival is reliant upon them being competent and strong.
- They think strangers will attack at any sign of weakness.
- Backing down or showing fear while being confronted reveals weakness and an inability to be socially adept.
- They'll remain silent if they have doubts about being safe to confront an issue.

Relating to my own situation, I was convinced my panic attacks and fretfulness were normal until I learned I was suffering from social and generalized anxiety disorder.

In the past, anxiety as a psychological disorder was not well-understood. Fortunately, with the advent of more advanced therapies it's possible to have a better understanding of and control over your emotions.

## Can You Control Your Anxiety?

***Absolutely!***

As I've mentioned, incorporating the tools and strategies I provide in this book will help you ***gain control over your emotions before they gain control over you.***

The strategies are the preparation of resources you use before or while taking action. They can be developed once you determine what caused your emotions to get out of control so you can be prepared for the next time they surface.

Because people tend to exhibit the same patterns of behaviors, thoughts or actions, a well-thought out plan can be put in place to manage them.

Earlier I discussed the six stages of changed behavior that include pre-contemplation, contemplation, preparation, action, maintenance and relapse. Following are five steps to help you manage those stages to be more effective, positive and in control:

**Step one:** Understanding these stages helps create an awareness of your situation.

**Step two:** Meditate on what you want to achieve, then redirect your thoughts to be positive instead of negative.

A negative thought can make you agitated and restless, instead of calm and peaceful. Anxiety feeds off negative thoughts that tear you down instead of building you up. Changing your mindset to thinking positively will build you up so you can achieve anything you want!

**Step three:** Commitment and determination to change. The only person who really can effectuate change in your life is you. So by reading this book you're taking your first steps toward understanding your kind of anxiety (and/or panic attacks), then creating solutions to conquer them.

**Step four:** Do the exercises and assignments in this book to institute change. Some strategies are so simple that people don't see their overall value.

However, the positive results that I personally and my clients have achieved is that they're highly effective when done with conviction, perseverance and commitment.

## Breathing Techniques to Calm Anxiety

The exercise in the previous chapter started you on a path to discovering what causes your particular type(s) of anxiety. For example, an event can be greatly influenced by how you perceive and interpret it (i.e., the approach you use to evaluate then explain your thoughts).

These breathing techniques can calm rapid heartbeats, and increase blood flow and oxygen to your entire body, which reduces over-stimulated responses to stress.

Through self-observation, and practicing breathing, relaxation, and meditative techniques, you'll begin to achieve positive results. You'll also notice that rigid thoughts will become more flexible. The possibility of change no longer feels impossible, and in fact will become second nature once the changes are acquired.

For this exercise you'll complete the following steps:

- While sitting or lying down, slowly count to four while inhaling air first into your abdomen then your chest all in one step.
- Hold your breath for four seconds while imagine feeling calm and relaxed. Then slowly exhale for four seconds.

- Repeat the exercise four to eight times while directing your attention to achieving a calm state of relaxation and controlling your thoughts. The more you do this exercise, the easier it will become.

Achieving a state of calm and relaxation doesn't happen by magic; it happens by observing what you're feeling and thinking. That time gap between inhaling and exhaling is your portal of recognition and achievement. Then exhaling allows those feelings to become part of your being.

How many times did you do this exercise today (no worries if you did it only once)? __________

Did you practice the technique of slow, deep breathing? _____ Yes _____ No

How was your mood during the exercise (i.e., excited, anxious, calm, nervous, etc.)?

_____________________________________________

Did you stay focused on the exercise?
_____ Yes _____ No

Were you thinking of something else?
_____ Yes _____ No

If yes, what were you thinking about?

_____________________________________________
_____________________________________________
_____________________________________________
_____________________________________________

How did you feel after you finished the breathing exercise, (visualize, then describe it)?

_______________________________________________

_______________________________________________

I'd like you to utilize these techniques as often as possible over the next week (and every week for that matter) while noting that inhaling and exhaling longer each time can strengthen your thoughts and breathing patterns.

Before you do this exercise write down how you feel, then how you feel after you do it, so you can observe how the benefits of oxygen and self-observation help you feel calmer and more relaxed.

## The Powers of Observation

**"You are now, and you do become,**
**what you think about."**
~**Earl Nightingale, author of *The Strangest Secret***

A good way to ease the burden of anxiety is to become aware of your symptoms. In other words, *what you see is what you know.*

Self-observation means living in the present reality, and not projecting non-existent "what-ifs" into a situation.

To clarify, you now know those strange feelings you experience have an actual name: *anxiety.* So going forward, your focus will be on observing your symptoms so you can name them, then choose the proper healing techniques (or a therapist if that's the route you choose).

For instance, instead of thinking *I'm nervous, anxious, distressed,* you can replace that with, *Now that I've determined I have anxiety, I can control it. I can also write my thoughts down while using the exercises in previous chapters.*

Managing your situation means being responsible for and owning that you have problems, and that they can be controlled with effort and diligence.

## Exercise 8: Journaling

All of the exercises I've included involve journaling as it's very beneficial to capture thoughts and feelings as they occur.

Commitment to your healing means participating in your well-being. Therefore, keeping a journal allows you to monitor the amount of anxiety you experience so you can see areas that need work.

During this exercise you'll write down what you feel during a moment of emotional imbalance, the amount of time it lasted, what might have caused it, and how you felt after it subsided.

Find a place that's safe and private so you won't be disturbed, and where you'll feel comfortable about sharing your feelings, even if it's just on paper.

Its objective is for you to observe, then write down your daily interactions from the moment you wake up for at least a two-week period. (You can create your own question and answer list by building on the following suggested prompts.):

How did you act when you talked on the phone to a family member, friend, colleague? (i.e., lovingly, nurturing, irritatingly, like you couldn't be bothered)?

______________________________________________

______________________________________________

______________________________________________

______________________________________________

______________________________________________

What kinds of positive or negative things did you say to them?

______________________________________________

______________________________________________

______________________________________________

______________________________________________

______________________________________________

If you're in a relationship, how did you interact with your spouse when you first woke up (i.e., did you joyfully say 'Good morning!'? Or did you get up in a bad mood and take it out on them?)

______________________________________________

______________________________________________

______________________________________________

______________________________________________

______________________________________________

If you have a pet, how did you treat it?

______________________________________________

______________________________________________

______________________________________________

______________________________________________

______________________________________________

During your interactions throughout the day, what kinds of thoughts crossed your mind (i.e., loving, frustrated, irritated, confused, worry, etc.)?

_______________________________________________

_______________________________________________

_______________________________________________

_______________________________________________

_______________________________________________

About who or what, and why?

_______________________________________________

_______________________________________________

_______________________________________________

_______________________________________________

_______________________________________________

Did you make excuses for your unkind or abrupt behavior? _____ Yes _____ No

If yes, why do you think that was? And what kinds of alternative positive thoughts could you have had?

_______________________________________________

_______________________________________________

_______________________________________________

_______________________________________________

_______________________________________________

Was it a negative or positive state of mind throughout most of the day? _______________________

How long did it last (a few minutes, a few hours, the entire day?) _______________________

If you went to work, how was your day?
_________ Good _______ Bad _____ Indifferent

Did you have any negative interactions with your boss or a co-worker? _____ Yes _____ No

If yes, do you know why that might have happened (i.e., they treated me harshly because they hate me, or are jealous of or intimidated by me. Or my boss treats everyone rudely, so it's not personal.)?

_______________________________________________

_______________________________________________

_______________________________________________

_______________________________________________

_______________________________________________

Do you constantly worry about what others think of you? _____ Yes _____ No

If yes, what kinds of things do you assume people think of you?

_______________________________________________

_______________________________________________

_______________________________________________

_______________________________________________

_______________________________________________

If you have children, do you constantly monitor and micromanage their behavior? _____ Yes _____ No

If yes, give some examples:

_______________________________________________

_______________________________________________

_______________________________________________

Do you think your family would be a complete mess without you? _____ Yes _____ No

Do you constantly show them that you trust and respect them? _____ Yes _____ No

Do you show them that you appreciate the things they do, and commend them for their actions? _____ Yes _____ No

If yes, what kinds of things do you do and say to show them how you feel?

_______________________________________________

_______________________________________________

_______________________________________________

_______________________________________________

_______________________________________________

Doing this exercise every day, then reviewing it at the end of each week, will give you a comprehensive overview of your behavior at work and at home so you can see behaviors that need to be changed.

## Daily Positive Affirmations

Napoleon Hill (the self-help author who wrote the iconic book, *Think and Grow Rich,* that's helped millions of people since its publication in 1937) said, "Whatever the mind can conceive and believe, it can achieve."

I firmly believe that the power of suggestion, and reframing how you perceive your problems, can prevent or at least get your anxiety under control.

After every day of journaling, saying positive affirmations provides emotional support to eliminate negative thoughts, and encourage positive ones to enter your mind more often.

Visualize and *comprehend the meaning* of each affirmative word as you recite them. Then incorporate them into your daily routine so they become second nature to you:

- I am not my feelings. I have feelings.
- I am not my thoughts. I have thoughts.
- I am not my emotions. I have emotions.
- I am not anxious. I have anxiety.

These are just a few examples as you can create affirmations that resonate with your specific situation.)

If you've never done this before, please don't discount the power of affirmations as they can have a profound effect on your emotional healing

You might feel uncomfortable doing this at first. But the longer you routinely do affirmations while fully absorbing and comprehending their meaning, the more you'll begin to see changes in your behavior, and how you see people and world around you.

**And that would be a grand thing to happen!**

# CONCLUSION

There's a fine line between anxiety and fear. People who learn to control their fears have fewer risks of experiencing anxiety even if they're vulnerable to their emotions.

As previously stated, fear is the perception that something is about to happen, but has yet to occur because it's in the future (or it might not happen at all).

Think about it this way: fear is a brick that begins to construct anxieties, phobias and low self-esteem. Removing (or better yet, crushing!) the brick eliminates the foundation underneath the wall on which negative emotions, worries and problems can be built.

Stress is a state of mental or emotional pressure resulting from very demanding circumstances such as a high workload. Planning your daily activities will keep your thoughts organized so you can say good-bye to stress and distress forever.

You have the power to change or eliminate *anxiety* altogether because it's a treatable condition. Whereas being *anxious* is a state of mind that can create problems, and take you totally by surprise. Understanding the difference between the different kinds of anxiety versus panic attacks can help you take control of your emotional, physical and cognitive behavior.

By incorporating the tools and techniques I suggest in this book, you can learn how to create a solution rather than overreacting to circumstances by...

- recognizing you have an anxiety.
- identifying it then giving it a name.
- putting it in its proper place (specifically, *I have anxiety, rather than I am anxious*).
- reflecting on your thoughts you had during an out-of-control situation, then writing them down to help you create a practical solution.
- practice, practice, and practice some more to allow your strategies to become second nature.

Making an honest effort and ongoing commitment to work on your problem will get you on the path to a calmer, more peaceful life. Your anxieties will lessen the closer you get to your goal.

***Never give up, and always have hope, as a better life is just around the corner!***

Thank you so much for joining me on this journey to self-discovery, awareness, acceptance, and ultimately joy and happiness!

With many blessings,

# REFERENCES

## Books

American Psychiatric Association. (2013): *Diagnostic and Statistical Manual of Mental Disorders*, (5th. Ed.). Washington, D.C.: American Psychiatric Publishing.

Anticich, S.A.J., P.M. Barret, R. Gillies, and W. Silverman (2012): *Recent Advances in Intervention for Early Childhood Anxiety. Australian Journal of Guidance and Counselling*, 22(2), 157- 172. doi: 10.1017/jgc.2012.24

Beck, A., G. Emery, and Ruth Greenberg (1985): *Anxiety Disorders and Phobias: A cognitive perspective*. Basics Books, Inc.

Bourne, PhD., E. J. (2015): *The Anxiety & Phobia Workbook,* (5th ed.). New Harbinger Publications, Inc., 6th edition.

Brewin, C. R. (2003): *Post-Traumatic Stress Disorder: Malady or myth?* Vail-Ballou Press.

Chartier, M.J., Walker, J.R., Stein, M.B. (2003). *Considering Comorbidity in Social Phobia.* Social Psychiatry and Psychiatric Epidemiology, 38:728–34.

Corsini, R. J., & Wedding, D. (2011): *Current Psychotherapies*. Brooks/Cole, Cengage Learning.

Demyttenaere, K., R. Bruffaerts, J. Posada-Villa, I. Gasquet, V. Kovess, J. P. Lepine, P.S. Wang, (2004): *Prevalence, Severity and Unmet Need for Treatment of Mental Disorders in the World Health Organization World Mental Health Surveys.* The Journal of the American Medical Association, 291(21), 2581-2590. doi: 10.1001/jama.291.21.2581.

DiClemente, C.C., S.K. Faihurst, M.M. Velasquez, J.O. Prochaska, W.F. Velicer, & J.S. Rossi, (1991): *The Process of Smoking Cessation: An analysis of pre-contemplation, contemplation, and preparation stages of change.* Journal of Consulting and Clinical Psychology, 59(2), 295-304.

Fricchione, G. (2004): *Generalized Anxiety Disorder.* New England Journal of Medicine, 351, 675-682. doi: 10.1056/NEJMcp022342

Heng, M., and J.A. Greenwald, J. A. (2007). *Toronto Notes 2007: A comprehensive medical reference.* Type & Graphics Inc.

Hersen, M., and M. Biaggio (2000). *Effective Brief Therapies: A clinician's guide.* Academic Press Limited.

Merriam-Webster's Collegiate Dictionary (10th ed.). Merriam-Webster, Inc., Massachusetts:

Merriam-Webster's Medical Dictionary (2016). Merriam-Webster, Inc., Massachusetts.

Metcalf, L., & Thomas, F. (1994). *Client and Therapist Perceptions of Solution-Focused Brief Therapy: A qualitative analysis.* Journal of Family Psychotherapy, 5(4), 49-66.

Sadock, B. J., and V.A. Sadock (2007): *Synopsis of Psychiatry. Behavioral sciences/clinical psychiatry,* (10th ed.). Lippincott Williams & Wilkins.

Willis, Mike (2012): *Anxiety in the Elderly.* Senior Behavioral Health Services (2012): 1-37. PDF file.

Young, M. E. (2013). *Learning the Art of Helping: Building blocks and techniques,* (5th ed.). Pearson.

## Websites

Anxiety and Depression Association of America (n.d.). Facts and Statistics.
Retrieved from
http://www.adaa.org/about-adaa/press-room/facts-statistics

*Any Anxiety Disorder Among Adults.* National Institute of Mental Health (n.d.).
Retrieved from
http://www.nimh.nih.gov/statistics/1ANYANX_ADULT.shtml

*A Report on Mental Illnesses in Canada.* Public Health Agency of Canada.
Retrieved from
http://www.phac-aspc.gc.ca/publicat/miic-mmac/chap_4-eng.php

Beck M.D., Aaron T. Pearson Clinical Psychology.
Retrieved from
http://www.pearsonclinical.com/psychology/authors/beck-aaron.html

Dvorsky, George (6 November 2013): *Are We in the Midst of an Anxiety Epidemic?* io9.
Retrieved from
http://io9.gizmodo.com/are-we-in-the-midst-of-an-anxiety-epidemic-1459542453

Eells, Josh (17 June 2015): *Emma Stone Talks 'Irrational Man,' the Sony Hack and Keeping Her Personal Life Private. The Wall Street Journal.*
Retrieved from
http://www.hollywoodreporter.com/features/emma-stones-battle-shyness-panic-attacks-phobias-way-oscars-968543

*Generalized Anxiety Disorder: When Worry Gets Out of Control.* National Institute of Mental Health.
Retrieved from
https://www.nimh.nih.gov/health/publications/generalized-anxiety-disorder-gad/index.shtml

Hamilton, M. (1959). *The Assessment of Anxiety States by Rating.* [Abstract] British Journal of Medical Psychology, 32, 50-55.
Retrieved from
http://scholar.google.ca/scholar

History of Mental Health Treatment (1800s to 2000s)
Retrieved from
http://www.dualdiagnosis.org/mental-health-and-addiction/history/

*Post-Traumatic Stress Disorder.* University of Maryland Medical Center.
Retrieved from
http://umm.edu/health/medical/altmed/condition/posttraumatic-stress-disorder

The WHO Word Mental Health Survey Consortium (2004).
Retrieved from
http://jama.jamanetwork.com/article.aspx?articleid=1988447

Watson, Kathryn (November 18, 2015): *What is Obsessive Personality Disorder?*
Retrieved from
http://www.healthline.com/health/obsessive-compulsive-personality-disorder?s_con_rec=false#Overview1

Yi, David (ND): *Glenn's Crusade: The actress is on a mission to end stigma against mental illness.*
Mashable.
Retrieved from
http://mashable.com/2016/01/25/glenn-close-mental-illness-stigma/#KhNIcXCNUgq3

# ESMERALDA FRANCO-MANSILLA
## Physician, Psychotherapist, and Mental Health Therapist

After graduating with a degree in medicine from the University of Nuevo Léon in Monterrey, Mexico, Esmeralda Franco-Mansilla received her Master's of Arts degree in Counseling Psychology from the Yorkville University in New Brunswick, Canada.

During the first years of her medical career, Esmeralda was a general physician (GP) in various remote mountain communities and villages throughout Colombia, South America. Though she moved to Canada, she never lost her desire to help others find ways to overcome their problems and personal setbacks.

Throughout her extensive career, Dr. Franco-Mansilla has dedicated herself to the practice of counseling and psychotherapy in behavioral science, and to diagnosing and treating different psychological pathologies in children, adolescents, teens and adults with various mental and anxiety disorders.

As a result of her extensive training and experience she developed cognitive behavior therapy and relaxation techniques to help her clients experience a better quality of life.

Known as a compassionate forward-thinker who prefers a more hands-on approach to wellness, Dr. Franco-Mansilla's strong sense of self-awareness, attentiveness and intuition helps her clients manage their anxiety in a more holistic, organic manner.

CORE COMPETENCIES

- Seasoned medical doctor South America with experience in general medicine, urgent care and minor surgeries as a family physician to all age groups.
- Health and mental services consultant.
- Private practice and online counselling services. January 2015 to Present.
- Social Worker Volunteer, London Employment Help Center, London, Ontario. July 2014 to August 2014. Assisted with the physical recovery and functionality of patients requiring complex care.
- Therapy Intern, Madame Vanier Children's Services, London, Ontario. September 2013 to June 2014. Consulted children and parents with emotional distress, then supported them in the process of behavioral pattern modification.
- From January 2008 to August 2013, Esmeralda assisted patients at the Cross Cultural Center and St. Joseph's Shelter, London, Ontario on medical issues. Plus acted as interpreter and translator whenever they had appointments with a doctor or at a hospital.

- Physician's Assistant, Family Physician Dr. David Hodder, London, Ontario. Interviewed, examined, then advised treatment alternatives for his patients. January 2003 to June 2006.
- Besides volunteering as an interpreter for Spanish patients in hospitals and clinics, I volunteered in Parkwood Hospital, London, Ontario, Canada in the Complex Care department from 2004 to 2005.
- Physician's Assistant, Arango's Clinic, McAllen, Texas. June 2001.
- Physician, Bogotá, Colombia and Monterrey, Mexico. 1990 to 2001.
- Interpreter and translator.

## ACHIEVEMENTS | COMMUNITY LEADERSHIP AND PHILANTHROPY

- Mental health counseling expertise.
- Anxiety management techniques (i.e., relaxation and cognitive behavior therapy).
- Incorporated patient care and health to create preventative programs.
- Phlebotomy, patient care and minor surgeries.
- Assisted individuals needing social adjustment and emotional re-balance.
- Achieved positive outcomes using cognitive behavioral interventions for stress and anxiety.

In addition to having a husband, two daughters and a son, Dr. Franco-Mansilla is a private practice psychotherapist in London, Ontario, Canada.

*(continue to next page for publications and contact information)*

PUBLICATIONS:

- Author of numerous articles on EzineArticles.com

- *Calmado, Confidado, Controlado (Calm, Confident, and Control)* that was originally written for the Spanish-speaking marketplace

To find out more about her therapy program, methodologies, and online consultation, you can contact her via esmermansillamd@gmail.com, or her profile page on LinkedIn.

www.ingramcontent.com/pod-product-compliance
Lightning Source LLC
Chambersburg PA
CBHW070131260726
48658CB00001B/359